STECK-VAUGHN

StartSmart
Connecting Learning to Life

Study Skills

Consultants

Jim Ford
Training Specialist
Center for Literacy Studies
University of Tennessee
Knoxville, Tennessee

Daniele D. Flannery, Ph.D.
Associate Professor of Adult Education
Coordinator: Adult Education D.Ed. Program
The Pennsylvania State University
Capital Campus—Harrisburg

Barbara Tondre-El Zorkani
Educational Consultant
Adult and Workforce Education
Austin, Texas

Harcourt Achieve
Rigby • Saxon • Steck-Vaughn

www.HarcourtAchieve.com
1.800.531.5015

Acknowledgments

Staff Credits

Executive Editor: Ellen Northcutt
Supervising Editor: Julie Higgins
Associate Editor: Sharon Sargent
Director of Design: Scott Huber
Associate Director of Design: Joyce Spicer
Designer: Jim Cauthron
Production Manager: Mychael Ferris
Production Coordinator: Paula Schumann
Image Services Coordinator: Ted Krause
Senior Technical Advisor: Alan Klemp
Electronic Production Specialist: David Hanshaw

Cover Illustration

Joan Cunningham

Photo Credits

P. 32 © Carolyn Wyman, reprinted by permission of Harcourt, Inc.; p. 44 ©Michael Newman/PhotoEdit. Additional photography by Comstock Royalty Free, Corbis Royalty Free, and Getty Images Royalty Free.

ISBN 0-7398-6020-8

Contents

To the Learner

Everybody can improve the way they study. By studying "smarter," you can understand more and get better grades. Steck-Vaughn's *Start Smart Study Skills* book will give you strategies to help you improve the way you study. By studying successfully, you'll be better able to achieve your educational and life goals.

Studying is a process that requires planning and preparation. Good study habits can help you learn more quickly and more efficiently. The strategies in this book will help you plan your studying and manage, research, and present information. Try all of the strategies and see which ones work best for you. Your favorites will help you again and again.

As you work through this book, be sure to:

- Fill out the **Identify Your Study Habits** chart on page 5. This will give you an idea of what your current study habits are.
- Write down your goals in the **Set Your Study Goals** web on page 7. Setting goals and checking your progress help you to stay motivated.
- Check out the **Tips** throughout this book. They provide a slightly different approach to the strategies.
- Complete the **Think About It** activities. These help you think about what you have learned. You'll also see the connection to everyday life.
- Create a **Journal.** This book is divided into four main topics. At the end of each topic, you will have the opportunity to write in your journal. Writing thoughts in your own words will help you remember what you've learned and help you track your progress.
- Review what you have learned by completing **What Works for You?** on page 48.

Identify Your Study Habits

This chart can help you learn about your current study habits. As you use the strategies in this book, you may notice that your habits are changing.

For each statement, circle A (always), S (sometimes), or N (never).

When I study, I . . .	always	sometimes	never
make a weekly plan to arrange my time.	A	S	N
set goals to focus my studying.	A	S	N
include review time in my study plan.	A	S	N
budget enough time to study.	A	S	N
take notes to organize my studying.	A	S	N
organize my information with visual aids.	A	S	N
test myself to check my progress.	A	S	N
focus my research.	A	S	N
make predictions to direct my research.	A	S	N
collect information from a wide variety of sources.	A	S	N
use an outline to organize information.	A	S	N
get ready to present information, whether through a test, research paper, or oral presentation.	A	S	N

Set Your Study Goals

*I will study and get ready
and perhaps my time will come.*

Abraham Lincoln (1809–1865)
16th President of the United States

Getting an education was not easy for Abraham Lincoln. During his childhood, he spent less than one year in school. Lincoln decided to study law as an adult. Often he had to walk miles to borrow the books he needed. But eventually, he did practice law before becoming a politician.

What are you getting ready for? Think about why you want to improve your study skills. Do you want to pass an important test? Do you need to collect information for a research paper? Perhaps improving your study skills will be one step to getting a better job. In your own words, explain why you wish to improve your study skills.

....

....

....

....

....

Consider how improving your study skills could help you in these areas of your life.

- **Family:** How could improving your study skills help make your family life better?
- **Work:** How could it help you find a better job or get a promotion?
- **Community:** How could it help you serve your community?
- **Self:** How could it help your education, the quality of your free time, or help you explore a new interest?

Write your goals for studying in the spaces below. Think about how having better study skills will affect your family, your work, your community, and yourself.

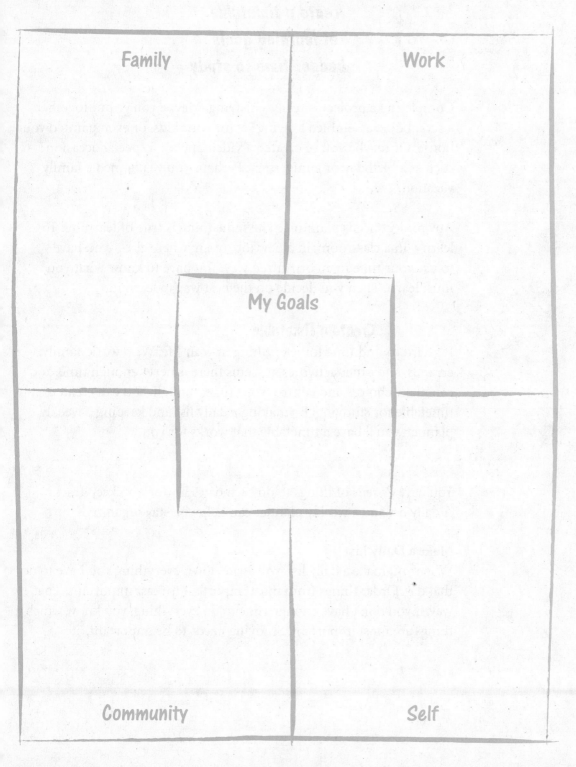

Family

Work

My Goals

Community

Self

Keep your goals in mind as you work through this book.

Topic 1: **Plan Your Studying**

In this section, you will learn how to:
- *create a timetable*
- *set learning goals*
- *budget time to study*

Completing a project is really satisfying. Maybe you've put together a scrapbook, assembled a swing set for your kids, or even painted your house. Or maybe you've created a videotape for a special occasion such as a birthday or anniversary. Perhaps you've planned a family vacation.

Any project needs planning. The same thing is true of learning. To learn—in a classroom, in a new job, or anywhere else—you have to use your time in an organized way. You have to know what you must learn. Then you decide on the best way to learn it.

Strategy 1: **Create a Timetable**
It's hard to find time for everything in your life. With work, family, errands, and other activities, it seems there is never enough time. You can make choices and control your time, though. You can create a timetable for studying. By making a daily list and keeping a weekly planner, you'll have a timetable that works for you.

Plan Your Time
You have dozens of things to do each day. How do you keep track? A daily list and a weekly planner can help you stay organized.

Make a Daily List
When you make a daily list, you write down everything you have to do that day. Order things from most important to least important. That way, if you don't have enough time to do everything, you know which things are most important. Studying needs to be important.

Ben wrote this daily list for Tuesday.

Tuesday
Work, 8-4
Lunch with Dewain
Coach baseball
Study
Pick up birthday present for my brother
Call Aunt Ruth to remind her about the party
Do laundry

By making a list, Ben kept track of the things he had to do.

Keep a Weekly Planner

Many people find it useful to plan their studying a week at a time. You can buy or make a planner that shows a week on each page. Each day is broken down into time periods. Use a daily list to help you fill out your weekly planner.

In the planner, write down anything you absolutely need to do that week. These would be things like work, picking up a child, and doctor's appointments. Include time each day for studying and write it down.

Having your study time written in your planner has two purposes. It lets you see when you are supposed to study. This makes it easier to stick with your plan. It also reminds you that studying is an important part of your day, every day.

For a 20-week planning calendar, see Steck-Vaughn's Start Smart Planner.

Hanna, a student taking an evening class, started to keep a weekly planner. Notice how she allowed time to study every day.

MONDAY	8:30—leave home 9—at work 12:30—lunch with Anne	5—off work 6:30—dinner 8-9:30—STUDY	10/7
TUESDAY	7:30—leave home 8—at work 12:30—lunch at desk, study till 1	5—off work 5-6—run errands 6:30—dinner 8-9:30—STUDY	10/8
WEDNESDAY	7:30—leave home 8—at work 12—lunch with brother 2—off work—run errands	3:30—pick up Jim ♡ 4—go to library to study 6—dinner with Jim 7—class in rm. 290	10/9
THURSDAY	8:30—leave home 9—at work 12—lunch, study till 1 2—off work—go shopping	3:30—pick up Jim 4—take Jim to soccer, study till 6 6:30—dinner 8-10—time with Jim ♡☺♡	10/10
FRIDAY	7:30—leave home 8—at work 12—lunch with Kathryn 2—off work	3:30—pick up Jim 4-6—run errands with Jim 6:30—dinner 8-9:30—study group at Brian's	10/11

Hanna's changing work schedule is hard to remember. Her planner helps her keep on track.

Hanna ends up studying at different times each day. She tries to study for more than an hour a day.

Try It Yourself

Plan your next week using the planner below. Put in your important responsibilities. Include time for studying each day.

MONDAY		DATE

TUESDAY		DATE

WEDNESDAY		DATE

THURSDAY		DATE

FRIDAY		DATE

How much time did you allow for studying each day? How much study time will you have for the week?

Think About It

How can you keep your schedule handy so you can add to it throughout the day?

....

....

....

Strategy 2: Set Learning Goals

Setting goals for yourself will keep you motivated. You are more willing to do what's needed if you can "keep your eye on the prize."

Your goal might be to pass the driving test on the first try. You might set a goal of getting an A in your word-processing course. You might decide to be the best student in your auto repair class. When you set learning goals, you give yourself something to aim for. You give your studying a purpose.

Decide What You Want

Think about why you are studying. Do you want to learn a skill? Do you want to get a particular job? Do you want to get a good score on a standardized test?

Don't just pick the first thing that comes into your mind. Think about it awhile. What do you really want? How will studying help?

Ji-Won decided that he was studying so he could get a better job. He asked himself why he wanted a new job. After he thought about it, he realized he wanted a new job so he would have more money to buy a better car. He also wanted more money so he could give his mother some help. His goal was to make more money.

Try It Yourself

Think about what you want and how studying will help. Write down all the ideas you can think of below. Then circle the idea that shows the main thing you really want. This is your goal.

....

....

....

Break Down Your Goals

Sometimes goals are hard to reach. Other times they are complicated and have a lot of parts. These are the goals that you need to break down into smaller goals. As you complete each smaller goal, you will be closer to your large goal.

A pyramid chart can help you break down your goals. The large goal goes at the top. On each tier below, you break down the goal into smaller goals. When the chart is complete, you work on accomplishing the smaller goals from the bottom up.

Eduardo used a pyramid chart to break down his goals this way:

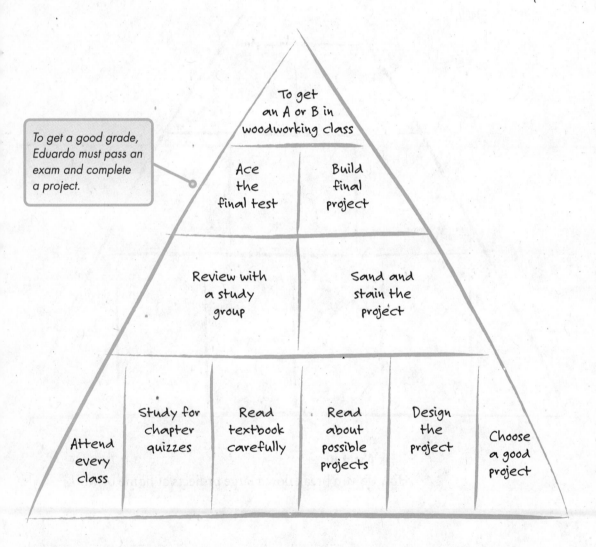

Each of the goals at the bottom of Eduardo's pyramid helps make the upper goals possible. The pyramid is a step-by-step plan for achieving a difficult or large learning goal.

For more information on setting goals, see Steck-Vaughn's Start Smart Goal Setting Strategies book.

Work with a Partner

Write down a large or difficult learning goal that you and your partner both share. (If you don't have a goal in common, do the exercise separately. Then compare notes.) In the pyramid below, break down the goal. Write down the smaller goals that will help you achieve your larger goal. Discuss which goals will be easier to accomplish and which will be more difficult.

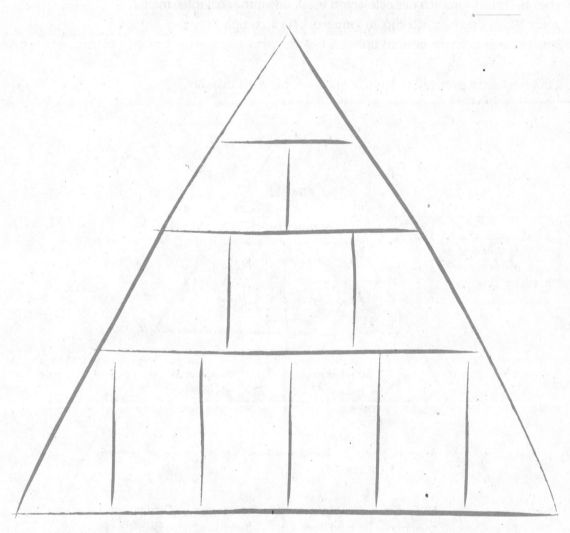

Think About It

How do you break down large projects at home or work?

....

....

....

Strategy 3: **Budget Time to Study**

You know your learning goals. You have a daily list and a weekly planner to help you stick to a timetable. Now you have to decide just how much time you need to budget for studying.

Just like you have a budget for money, you can have a budget for time. A money budget lets you see how much you can spend, like at the grocery store. When you budget time, you see how much time you can spend on something, like studying. You figure out ways to budget extra time for a "must-do" big project.

Eduardo knew what he needed to do to get a good grade in his woodworking class. He had to plan a project and build it. He also needed to read the textbook and take chapter quizzes.

Eduardo wrote down the tasks related to his learning goals. Next to each one, he estimated the amount of time he thought it would take to finish it.

1. Go to class every week—12 hours
2. Read the textbook—5 hours
3. Review for chapter quizzes—1 hour
4. Research possible projects—2 hours
5. Choose a good project—1 hour
6. Design the project—2 hours
7. Review for the test with a study group—2 hours
8. Sand and stain the project—3 hours
9. Build the final project—8 hours
10. Study for the final exam—2 hours

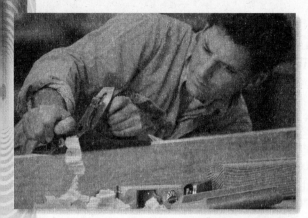

Eduardo's total estimated time for doing the tasks was 38 hours. The woodworking class was held over 12 weeks. Once he figured this out, he knew how much time to set aside for studying each week. He looked over his schedule in his weekly planner. Then he adjusted the planner so he had the right amount of study time.

To budget time, first figure out how long it will take to achieve your learning goals. Then set aside a reasonable amount of study time in your timetable. Once you've budgeted enough time for studying, your chances of success will be much greater.

To get the most out of your study time, decide what time of day you work best. Some people are most alert in the morning. Others work better after dinner. If possible, plan to study at the time of day you are most alert. Try not to study when you are very hungry or tired.

You should also try to study in a place that is quiet and comfortable. A room at home where you can shut out distractions, a desk in the library, or the kitchen table will do. Have the supplies you need close at hand. Put textbooks, notebooks, pens, paper, and a dictionary where you can reach them easily. You don't want to have to stop your studying to find what you need.

Many people need breaks when they study. If this would help you, budget extra time in your planner. Usual breaks are 15 minutes for each hour you study.

Work with a Partner
Go back to the pyramid chart you created with your partner on page 14. Separately, decide on the amount of time each small goal will take. Write a list of goals and times on your own paper.

Now think about how long you have to achieve your larger goal. Compare your times to your partner's. For any times that are different, talk about why you thought the task would take that long. Is there anything you can learn from each other?

Think About It

How do you balance study time and free time in your life?

....

....

....

When You Plan Your Study Time

- Create a timetable for studying. Keep a daily list and a weekly planner to help you stick to your schedule.
- Set learning goals. If the goals are large, break them down into smaller goals.
- Budget time to study. Plan exactly how much time you will need for studying.

Journal

Write a paragraph about the way you planned your study time in the past. If you did not really plan the time, just write about the amount of time you studied and when. Then write a paragraph about some new ways you will plan your studying. Be as specific as possible.

Next, look at the goals you set on page 7. Note your progress for each of your goals. If you've achieved a goal, put a check next to it and congratulate yourself!

Topic 2: **Manage Information**

In this section, you will learn how to:
- *take notes*
- *improve memory skills*
- *check your progress*

When you study, you often have a lot of material to learn. Just reading or listening to the material is not enough. You have to find ways to manage the information you are learning.

Managing information means helping the important parts sink in. It also means arranging information in ways that make sense. Then you will be able to remember what you learn and use it in projects, papers, or tests. You can also manage information by going that extra mile and testing yourself to see what you can recall.

Strategy 1: **Take Notes**
When you take notes, you are doing more than putting words on paper. You are reacting to what you hear in class or read from a textbook. After you listen or read, you decide what information is important. You think about the important parts. You put it in order and write it down. All of this helps important information sink in.

Take Notes While Listening and Watching

When you listen to a lecture or a speech, it helps to take notes. Here are some tips:

TIP

Draw pictures or diagrams in your notes. It may help you visualize a new idea.

1. **Keep a record** — At the top of the page, write the class or topic, the speaker's name, and the date.

2. **Attend class regularly** — Notes you get from a friend are not as good as notes you take yourself.

3. **Sit front and center** — You will be able to see better, hear better, and are less likely to be distracted.

4. **Listen actively** — Don't write down every single thing the speaker says. Think about what is being said and write down what is most important. Keep your mind working, and don't be a note-taking robot!

5. **Listen for word signals** — Speakers often give cues about what's important by repeating information, speaking more quickly or loudly, writing it on the board, or using phrases such as
   - "The most important event was . . . ."
   - "You will need to know . . . ."
   - "Two points to remember are . . . ."

6. **Leave plenty of space** — Always leave space in your notes to add things later. If you miss some information, fill in the gaps after the lecture. If you're not sure of something, ask the speaker or classmates.

7. **Examples are helpful** — Write down all examples and everything the speaker writes on the board.

8. **Review your notes** — Spend ten minutes after class reviewing your notes. You can change, organize, add, delete, summarize, or clarify what you wrote.

Sometimes you'll need to get information from a film or video. You may find it challenging to take notes while watching a moving picture. The viewing guide shown below is a helpful way to organize your thoughts as you watch. It gives you four ways to categorize information: ideas to hold onto, surprises, concerns, and questions. After you watch, you can then revisit your notes as needed. Of course, you can change any of the categories so the viewing guide meets your needs better.

Anne made these notes as she watched a documentary on heart disease.

Ideas to hold onto:	**Surprises:**
Fats provide energy & building materials for the body. Cholesterol = fat like substance in all animals, including humans.	Cholesterol and fat are <u>not</u> the same. Need fats to absorb some vitamins. Polyunsaturated fat → good
Concerns:	**Questions:**
More cholesterol in blood = more likely to have heart attacks. Since too much fat & cholesterol → heart disease, it's important to know what's in my food.	How can I keep from eating more than 65 grams of fat/day? How much fat do my favorite chips have? 

From "The Brain and Learning Facilitator's Guide" by Bonnie Benesh, Margaret Arbuckle, Pam Robbins, and Marcia D'Arcangelo, Alexandria, VA.: Association for Supervision and Curriculum Development. © 1998 ASCD.

If you are listening to a lecture or speech with lots of visual aids (such as illustrations, charts, or graphs), you can use split-page notes. Split-page notes allow you to copy graphics on one side and then write notes about them on the other.

Laura wanted to become a dog trainer. She went to a lecture on training puppies. She had her lined paper and a pencil to take notes. At the top, she wrote the date and the speaker's name. Her notes looked like this.

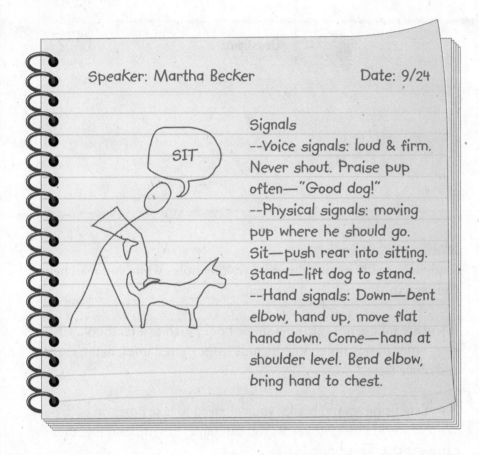

Speaker: Martha Becker   Date: 9/24

SIT

Signals
--Voice signals: loud & firm. Never shout. Praise pup often—"Good dog!"
--Physical signals: moving pup where he should go. Sit—push rear into sitting. Stand—lift dog to stand.
--Hand signals: Down—bent elbow, hand up, move flat hand down. Come—hand at shoulder level. Bend elbow, bring hand to chest.

The notes are drawn on one side of the page and written on the other side.

Laura gave this section of her notes the heading "Signals." This is the main idea. Under the heading, she used dashes to show supporting details. She put in a drawing to help her remember one of the signals. Her notes helped her remember the signals used to train puppies.

Try It Yourself

Use the viewing guide chart on page 22 to take notes while watching a TV show. If possible, have members of your family or friends take notes as well. Afterwards, compare your charts. Discuss how easy or hard it was to use the chart. Discuss other ways to organize your notes.

Ideas to hold onto:	Surprises:
Concerns:	Questions:

Take Notes While Reading

Studying usually involves reading. Taking notes while you read helps you remember what you have read.

If you are taking notes from a single book, such as a textbook, write your notes in one notebook. Include important names, dates, events, and other facts.

If you are using several books, you will need to take notes on each book. Write the notes on note cards. You can paperclip or band together the cards for the same book.

Here are some tips on taking notes while reading:

- Do not copy the words directly from the book. Restate the information in your own words.
- Use outlines, charts, or diagrams to help you organize information and make it easier to learn.
- You may want to take notes in a question-and-answer form, such as: *What is the main idea? The main idea is . . . .*
- Make a list of unfamiliar words, look them up in the dictionary, and write down their meanings in your own words.

Try It Yourself

Choose a textbook or manual. Read a section or a chapter of the book as though you need to understand it for class. Write notes on the important ideas and details.

After you have finished your note taking, read over your notes. Add any missing information. Look up any words you do not know. Did your note taking help you understand and remember what you read?

Think About It

How can you practice note taking so it becomes easier over time?

....

....

....

TIP

Highlight the most important information with a colored highlighting pen.

Strategy 2: Sharpen Memory Skills

Imagine that you have a big test coming up. You've done the reading and taken good notes. How can you be sure you will remember all the important information?

Here are some ways to help you remember important information.

- **Say the information out loud.** Hearing information in addition to reading it gives your brain a chance to process it in a new way.
- **Try to visualize the information.** Read a fact, close your eyes, and try to see it on paper. "Seeing" the information in this way gives your brain a new way to process it.
- **Create an acronym.** This is a word made from the first letters of the words you must remember. For example, if you wanted to remember the names of the Great Lakes, you could create the acronym **HOMES.** The names of the Great Lakes are **H**uron, **O**ntario, **M**ichigan, **E**rie, and **S**uperior.
- **Color code your material.** Use different colored pens, highlighters, or stickie notes to mark different kinds of information.
- **Use rhymes to help you memorize.** The rhyme "*i* before *e*, except after *c*, and when sounding like *a*, as in *neighbor* or *weigh*" has helped many people spell correctly.

- **Use memory games.** Try thinking of a phrase using the first letters of words you need to remember. For years, people have memorized the names of the planets by using the silly sentence "**M**y **v**ery **e**ducated **m**other **j**ust **s**ent **u**s **n**ine **p**izzas." The first letters of each word stand for Mercury, Venus, Earth, Mars, Jupiter, Saturn, Uranus, Neptune, and Pluto.

Randy was studying to be a landscaper. He had to memorize a list of evergreen trees that grow in full sun. His list included cypress, holly, magnolia, araucaria, spruce, and pine. He tried two different methods to memorize his list.

First he created a sentence using words that start with the first letters of the words on his list:

> **C**ats **h**ave **a**lways **s**cared **m**eek **p**eople.

Then he created an acronym, a word made from the first letters of the words on his list:

CHAMPS

Try It Yourself
Imagine that you have to remember these tree names.

    ash   tupelo   hawthorne   snowbell   sycamore

Write a sentence in the space below to help you remember.

....

....

....

Now write an acronym to help you remember.

....

What other methods can you think of to help you remember these trees?
Write your ideas below.

....

....

....

....

....

Think About It
How do you already use memory aids in your life?

....

....

....

Strategy 3: Check Your Progress
As you study, you may wonder how well you are "digesting" the material.
You can check your progress with review sheets and self-tests.

Create a Review Sheet
To create a review sheet, go back over your notes and your reading.
Decide what information is the most important. It's kind of like
sending a telegram. People put only the most important information
in a telegram because they pay for each word. While you can use as
many words as you want, try to choose only the most important,
as though you were paying for each one.

On your review sheet, write names, dates, events, and instructions.
Then pick any other information you think is very important.

Lindita created a review sheet to help her study for her class on elder care. She included the following information.

Elders' Homes Need Changes/Safety
Bathrooms: support rails and grab bars, bathing chair or bench, nonskid mats, hand-held shower head.
Stairways: stair rails or ramps, light switches at top and bottom.

Financing for Elders' Homes
FHA for rural homes
Medicare/Medicaid for medical equipment
Local agencies

Lindita's sheet gave her the chance to review what changes should be made to make elders' homes safe. It also reminded her of the ways to pay for those changes.

Work with a Partner
Choose a class subject that you are part way through. Create a review sheet on the information covered so far. Exchange sheets with your partner. Does the review sheet make sense? Based on the review sheet, ask each other more questions. Should any other information be added to the review sheet?

....

....

....

....

Take a Self-Test
A self-test helps you test yourself on your study material. While it won't be the same as a real exam, it does let you know if you need to study more. Have you ever tried the blood pressure cuff at a drug store? It's not the same as a doctor's exam, but it does give you a "heads up." A self-test can give you a heads up on whether you've learned what you need to know.

To create a self-test, write questions about the material. If you know the format of the actual test that will be used, use that same format. Questions could be multiple choice, fill in the blank, short answer, essay, or a combination. Include questions on every piece of information you think is important.

Wait a day or two after creating the self-test, then take the test. Write your answers as if you were taking an actual test. Finally, check your answers by going back over your material. The questions you get wrong will show you what you need to study more.

Scott created and took this self-test for his class on first aid.

1. A dislocation is <u>a joint whose ball is out of its socket.</u>

2. Name three symptoms of shock.

   1. <u>Skin is pale, cool, & clammy.</u>

   2. <u>Pulse is weak and fast.</u>

   3. ....

3. How do you treat a small burn? <u>If a burn is less than half a square inch, cool the skin with cold water for ten minutes. Apply a sterile bandage—no creams.</u>

After he took the self-test, Scott realized that he needed to study some more. He could not name three symptoms of shock. He was pleased, though, to see that he answered the other questions correctly.

Try It Yourself

Create a self-test on a subject you are studying. After you answer the questions, go over your answers. What do you need to study further?

....

....

TIP

Trade self-tests with a friend or study partner.

Think About It

How do you know when you understand the material you're studying?

....

....

....

When You Manage Information

- Take notes on the information you need to study.
- Use graphics to help you organize information.
- Sharpen your memory using a variety of strategies.
- Check your progress with review sheets and self-tests.

Journal

Write a paragraph in your journal about which strategies for managing information were helpful to you. Tell how you might use the strategies in your everyday life.

Next, look at the goals you set on page 7. Note your progress for each of your goals. If you've achieved a goal, put a check next to it and congratulate yourself!

Topic 3: **Research Information**

In this section, you will learn how to:
- *focus your research topic and make predictions*
- *collect information*

You may have to go beyond the information in your textbooks when you study. Looking for additional information is called research. When you are researching a topic, you have lots of choices. You decide what to look up. You decide how best to use your time. You decide where to go for information and the exact information you need.

Strategy 1: Focus Your Topic

When you begin your research, focus your topic so you can cover the essential points in your paper or presentation.

Consider the following.

- **Think about how much and what kind of information you need.** This will depend on the type of assignment, such as a three-page essay or five-minute presentation. What can be covered in the space or time allotted?

- **Decide on an appropriate topic that will meet your audience's needs.** Sometimes the topic will be assigned.

- **Narrow this down to a particular aspect of the topic.** If you were writing about TV, you might focus on how TV affects children.

- **Then narrow this further so you can focus on your main idea.** You might decide to write about how watching violence on TV increases children's aggressive behaviors.

Your next step is to identify specific questions and issues to learn more about. Identify these before beginning your research efforts. You will often find that you will uncover more questions and issues as you do your research.

Betty volunteered to write a newsletter article for the PTA at her son's school. The PTA needed an article that would help parents select a day-care center. She followed the steps to focus her topic.

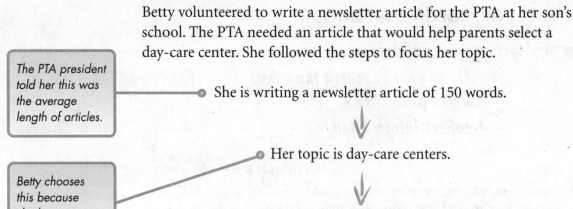

The PTA president told her this was the average length of articles.

She is writing a newsletter article of 150 words.

Betty chooses this because she knows many parents have this concern.

Her topic is day-care centers.

She narrows this down to the particular aspect of how to choose a good day care.

Betty is following a format often used for newsletter articles.

She then narrows this down to the top ten questions parents should ask a day-care provider. In her article, she will provide the questions and the answers. She will need to do more research, but now she has a focused topic.

Try It Yourself

Think of a topic you want to research. You may be interested in this topic because of your work or because you want to help your child with a homework project. Use the process outlined above to focus your chosen topic.

Use What You Know to Make Predictions

Jenny studies cosmetology, the study of hair, skin, and nail care. She needs to write a paper on one aspect of the history of cosmetology. Jenny writes what she knows or has learned about it from class. Then she writes what she knows from personal experience. She can use these notes to focus her topic.

Her notes look like this:

What I know: *Cosmetology was around in ancient times. Egyptians and Romans were especially big on skin care and baths. They did not have the same scientific knowledge we have today.*

What I have experienced: *My textbook goes into Egyptians and makeup. My face lotion says, "From the ancient Egyptian recipe."*

My predictions: *Recipes and discoveries from ancient Egypt may have affected today's practice of cosmetology. Ancient Egyptians used henna to decorate their hands and feet. This is probably similar to henna tattoos people use today.*

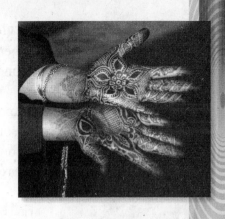

Jenny's predictions gave her research one clear direction with two possible branches. The clear direction was researching the skin-care practices of the ancient Egyptians. The first branch was finding out how Egyptian skin-care practices have affected modern cosmetology. The second branch was comparing products used in ancient Egypt with products used today.

Try It Yourself

Think of a topic with which you have some experience. Write any information you already know about the topic. Write what you have experienced about the topic. Use key words or short phrases. Use what you have written to make two predictions. Think about which predictions would make a good research paper.

Topic:

What I know: ....

....

....

What I have experienced: ....

....

....

My predictions:

1. ....

....

2. ....

....

Think About It

How do you begin to narrow down a topic?

....

....

Strategy 2: **Collect Information**

Where can you go to find the information you need? Your textbook is one place, but it's good to be aware of other resources.

Sometimes you are required to collect information from a variety of sources. Sources are books, Internet articles, people, and any other resources you use to get information. No matter where you live, there are resources available to help you find the information you need.

Find Books at the Library

Libraries list the books they have in cataloging systems. Some of these systems are on computers. Others are kept on cards in files. Every library catalogs books using the same system. Books are listed by author, title, and subject. They also have numbers or letters that tell you where to find them in the library.

Start with what you know: the title of the book, the author's name, or the subject you are researching. Searching by subject usually gives you the most choices. Here are some clues for looking up books.

TIP

Some titles begin with an abbreviation, such as Dr. or Mr. These are alphabetized as if the abbreviation were spelled out: Doctor, Mister.

- **Title:** Titles are listed alphabetically. The words *The, A,* and *An* are not part of the alphabetization.

- **Author:** Authors are listed alphabetically by last name.

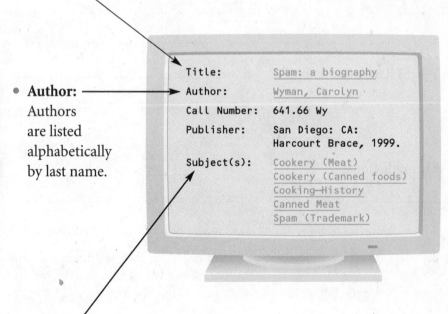

Title:	Spam: a biography
Author:	Wyman, Carolyn
Call Number:	641.66 Wy
Publisher:	San Diego: CA: Harcourt Brace, 1999.
Subject(s):	Cookery (Meat)
	Cookery (Canned foods)
	Cooking—History
	Canned Meat
	Spam (Trademark)

- **Subject:** Subjects are listed alphabetically. A book may be listed under more than one subject.

Jessica was trying to find a book on cooking for large groups of people. She did not know the name of a particular book. Therefore she did a subject, or key word, search under "catering."

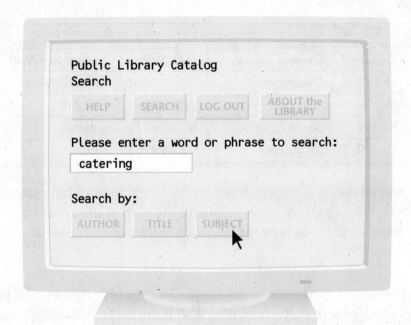

If Jessica's library used a card catalog, the same information would have been listed in the subject cards.

Jessica's search on "catering" gave her these results.

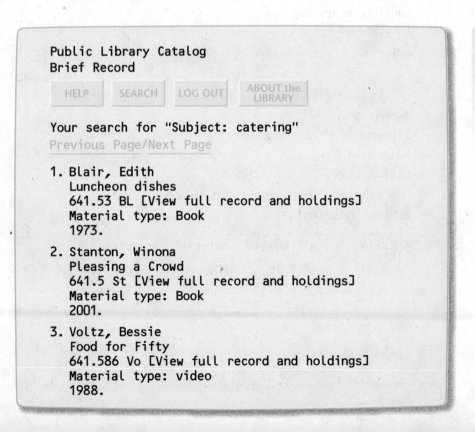

The Brief Record shows:
- the author's name
- the book title
- the call number
- the type of material
- the publication date

Notice the call number for each of the books. This number tells you where to find the book. Nonfiction library books are organized by the Dewey Decimal System. For a lot of research, you will need nonfiction books.

Dewey Decimal System			
000–099	General Works	500–599	Science and Math
100–199	Philosophy	600–699	Technology
200–299	Religion	700–799	Fine Arts
300–399	Social Sciences	800–899	Literature
400–499	Language	900–999	History

Fiction books are arranged alphabetically by the author's last name. Biographies, which are books telling the life story of someone, are arranged alphabetically by the last name of the person the book is about.

Jessica wanted more information about *Pleasing a Crowd,* so she clicked on [View full record and holdings]. This is the next screen she saw.

Jessica can check this book out at the North Library.

If Jessica is not at the North Library, she can click here to ask the library system to send the book to her library for free.

Public Library Catalog
Full Record

| HELP | SEARCH | LOG OUT | ABOUT the LIBRARY |

Previous Page/Next Page

Record #2
Title: Pleasing a Crowd
Author: Stanton, Winona
Call Number: 641.5 St
Publisher: Orlando: Harcourt, 2001.
Subject Heading(s): catering

Location	Call Number	Material	Status
Central	641.5 St	BOOK	Checked Out
North	641.5 St	BOOK	Available

Request Title

HELP WINDOW

Try It Yourself

In your local library, find three books on one of the following subjects. Write the titles, authors, and call numbers of each of the three books. Use the call numbers to locate the books in the library.

Circle one subject to look up: house painting
trade unions
lawn care

Title, author, and call number of three books on the subject:

1. Title: ....

   Author: ....

   Call Number: ....

2. Title: ....

   Author: ....

   Call Number: ....

3. Title: ....

   Author: ....

   Call Number: ....

TIP
If you can't find what you're looking for, ask a librarian for help.

Consider Other Library Resources

Libraries contain more than fiction and nonfiction books. The reference section includes many resources that you might find helpful.

- **Encyclopedias.** An encyclopedia has articles on subjects that are arranged alphabetically. Some, like *Encyclopedia Britannica*, are general. Others focus on specialized subjects, such as history, art, or sports.
- **Almanacs and yearbooks.** Almanacs and yearbooks give facts and statistics about government, economics, sports, and other topics. They are updated each year.
- **Atlases.** Atlases contain maps. They may also have historical and statistical information.
- **Audiovisual materials.** Many libraries have videotapes, DVDs, audiocassettes, and CDs you can borrow.

- **Magazines and newspapers.** Many libraries keep magazines and newspapers. Sometimes you can find back issues on microfilm or microfiche. You can look at these on a special machine.
- ***Readers' Guide to Periodical Literature.*** The *Readers' Guide* lists articles published each month in dozens of different magazines. To find an article, look in the volume covering the months you are interested in. Look up the author's name, if you know it. You can also search by subject. The *Readers' Guide* will tell you the name of the article. It will list the magazine and the month the article was published.
- **Dictionaries and thesauruses.** These reference books will help you use words better. Dictionaries tell you meanings and pronunciations. Thesauruses list synonyms—words that mean the same as other words.

TIP
The Readers' Guide is most useful if you are looking for up-to-date information.

Julia looked in her library's reference section to find information on wallpapering. She found help in the following resources.

- An encyclopedia. She found a book called *The Encyclopedia of Home Design.*
- The *Readers' Guide to Periodical Literature.* She found five recent articles about wallpapering methods.

Work with a Group
Each person should use the library's reference section. Without sharing information with others, find three reference resources about how to develop your own photographs.

....

....

....

As a group, compare the resources you listed. How many are different? Discuss how hard or easy it was to find the resources.

Use the Internet

There is a huge amount of information on the Internet. You can connect to the Internet on most public library computers if you do not have a computer yourself.

Logging onto the Internet is like walking into a candy store as a kid. You have so many choices. Lots of things look good. How can you ever decide? Narrowing down your choices can be hard. Not everything found on the Internet is reliable. For your research, you need information that is helpful and accurate.

TIP
Web sites by government agencies, universities, and trade and professional associations are usually reliable.

After you connect to the Internet, these steps can help you find what you need:

- **Choose a search engine.** A search engine shows you many Web sites that have information related to your search subject. To use a search engine, type in its Internet address. Some engines to try are *Yahoo* (http://www.yahoo.com) and *Google* (http://www.google.com). You can also try a metasearch engine, such as *Dogpile* (http://www.dogpile.com). A metasearch engine uses many different search engines to look for your subject.

- **Decide on specific words to search that will get you the information you need.** Say you are looking for information on training to become a plumber. You might type *plumbers* into the search box. Then your search engine would probably list Web sites on plumbing businesses, books about plumbers, and plumbing supply shops as well as sites on plumber training. If you type in *plumber training*, you are more likely to get the Web sites that you need.
- **Choose the Web sites that are most likely to be helpful.** Each Web site listed by a search engine will include a short description. Skim the descriptions. You can often tell which sites will be most useful from the descriptions.
- **Go to the most promising Web sites by clicking on their links (one at a time).** If you find a site with useful information, take notes. You can also print out pages from the Web site. If you are using your own computer, "bookmark" the site so you can easily return to it.

Brian looked up information on plumber training. He wanted to find out how to become a plumber. Brian found many Web sites during his search. Here are three Web sites he went to for more information:

He noted the
- Web site name
- Web site address
- and a description of the Web site

1. The Distance Learning Partnership
   www.dlpartnership.com
   Online training for the plumbing and heating professional.

2. Career Descriptions – Plumber
   www.careerdescriptions.com/plumber
   Plumbers install and repair sanitation, drainage, and water pipes . . . .

3. Becoming a Carpenter, Electrician, HVAC Technician, or Plumber
   www.pipesandheat.com
   Career options. Becoming a carpenter, electrician, HVAC . . . .

TIP
Check a Web site's links. Sometimes the links will be more useful than the original Web site.

Try It Yourself

Connect to the Internet using a computer at home, at school, or at your local library. Use a search engine to look for information on a topic you are studying. Visit Web sites until you find one that is helpful. Write the Web site's name and address below. Take notes on the information given at the Web site.

Web site name: ....

Web site address: ....

Notes: ....

....

....

Look into Other Resources

There are still more places you can go to find information that will help you in your research. Try the following sources.

- **Experts.** No matter what you are studying, there will be people who are experts at it. To find an expert, look in the phone book's white or Yellow Pages. You can also use a community college or university directory. Call or write to the expert. Talk to him or her about your subject. Take notes on what the expert tells you.
- **Government agencies.** There are government agencies at the local, state, and federal levels. They deal with subjects from social services to the environment. To get the address or phone number of a local

or state agency, look in the phone book or in the *National Directory of State Agencies* in your local library. To find a federal agency, look on the Internet under *A–Z Index of Federal Departments and Agencies*. You can also find information in the *United States Government Manual* at your local library. Many agencies send out free brochures, booklets, or information sheets.

Try It Yourself

Find contact information for an occupation you're in now or one that interests you. Write the contact information below.

....

....

....

How did you find this information? What other resources could you use?

....

....

Think About It

What do you do first when you need to find an expert?

....

....

....

When You Research

- Ask questions that will help you focus your research.
- Make predictions that will show you the direction to take.
- Collect information on your topic from various sources.

Journal

Write a few paragraphs as though you were writing to a friend. Tell the friend some of the key information you learned about research. Ask if the friend ever realized where to find information. Mention two new strategies that you are going to try the next time you need to research something.

Next, look at the goals you set on page 7. Note your progress for each of your goals. If you've achieved a goal, put a check next to it and congratulate yourself!

Topic 4: Present Information

In this section, you will learn how to:

- *organize information*
- *write a research paper*
- *give an oral presentation*
- *take a test*

You have a purpose when you research a topic. Your purpose is the reason you are doing the research in the first place. You might be researching so you will do well on a test. You may be doing research for a research paper. You could also be doing research for an oral presentation.

Your purpose will tell you how to present your information. On a test, you will give information to answer questions. In a research paper, you will use information to make a point or answer a question. For an oral presentation, such as a speech, you share information with a group of people.

Strategy 1: Organize Information

You have collected information and taken notes. Now it's time to organize the information and interpret its meaning.

In some ways, research is like putting together a big puzzle. You have collected the individual puzzle pieces of information. Now you group them into similar categories, like by color or straight edge for the puzzle border. Once you put the puzzle together, you can see what the pieces add up to. The interpretation is seeing the meaning, or the big picture.

Use an Outline

An outline breaks down the parts of your topic in a clear, organized manner. Writing an outline *before* beginning your paper or speech is helpful in organizing your thoughts. If your outline is good, your paper or speech should be easy to write.

> **TIP**
> *Brainstorm before you begin your outline. List all the ideas you want to include.*

Jenny, the cosmetology student, finished researching for her paper on Egyptian makeup. Now she needed to arrange her information and get ready to write. To organize her thoughts, she wrote the following outline.

Step 1: Write your topic at the top. This is the beginning of your introduction.

I. **Topic:** Although we may think of cosmetics as a modern invention, the ancient Egyptians used many products that are similar to what we use today.

II. The L'Oreal company and the French Museum's Research Laboratory have discovered how the Egyptians made their eye makeup.

Step 2: Write the main ideas you want to cover.

   A. This research shows Egyptians were highly skilled scientists.

III. Egyptians used a wide variety of cosmetics still in use today.

Step 3: Write details that support the main points.

   A. eye makeup

   B. skin creams and oils

   C. henna for hands and feet

   D. red powder for lips

IV. Studying the cosmetic practices of the ancient Egyptians helps us not only appreciate the past, but also better understand our own makeup.

Step 4: Write a conclusion. It should restate your topic and not introduce any new information.

Jenny first defined the topic she was going to write about. Then she broke down her information into main ideas and supporting details. Finally, she wrote a concluding sentence that stated her topic again. Afterwards, she edited her outline to make sure each of her points was covered. She wanted to make sure her paper would cover her topic well.

If Jenny was going to give a speech on Egyptian cosmetics, she could have used the same outline. Whether you're writing a research paper or giving an oral presentation, an outline can help you organize your material and prepare for the presentation of your research.

Outlining your material can also help you study for a test. Organizing your study materials can help you make connections and remember details.

TIP

Before you write, think about your audience. What do they want to know? What kinds of detail do they want?

Try It Yourself

Think of a subject you know a lot about. Outline three ideas on this topic you'd like to share with others.

I. ....

   A. ....

   B. ....

   C. ....

II. ....

   A. ....

   B. ....

   C. ....

III. ....

   A. ....

   B. ....

   C. ....

Strategy 2: Write a Research Paper

A research paper is a big project. Be sure to allow enough time to do it well. To increase your chance of getting a good grade, work on it steadily before it's due.

Your instructor will tell you how the paper should look. These basic steps will help you put together a good research paper.

1. **Read and research**—in the library, on the Internet, and with other resources.
2. **Take notes on the information you find.** Put your notes on index cards. Be sure to note the source of the information on each card. Write the title, author's name, publisher, place and date of publication, and page number where the information was found. For a Web site, write the Internet address, the Web site author (if there is one), and the date (if there is one).
3. **Create an outline.** Organize the information from your note cards.

4. **Write a first draft.** Get your thoughts down. Include an opening paragraph that states the main point of your paper. End with a closing paragraph that summarizes your main points.
5. **Revise your paper.** Make changes to make your writing smoother. Check for mistakes in grammar, spelling, and punctuation.
6. **Proofread your report.** Check it again. Correct any mistakes you find.
7. **Add a bibliography, if required.** A bibliography is a list of the sources you used to find your information. Creating a bibliography gives credit to your sources. Your instructors will give you the bibliography format they want you to use. Be sure to follow it carefully.
8. **Make a final, clean copy of your paper.**

Ben knew he would have to plan far ahead for his research paper. He worked long hours at his job and did not have much time for school work. He also had children to take care of. Because his paper was a huge part of his grade, Ben wanted to do a really good job. So he wrote down a plan on his calendar. He started with the day the paper was due and worked backward. He also plugged in his 12-hour shifts at work since he knew he couldn't work on the paper then.

Ben's calendar looked like this.

S	M	T	W	Th	F	S
1 Finish collecting all sources of information	2 Start writing note cards	3 12-hour shift, no study time	4 Do more note cards	5 Finish note cards, start outline	6 Finish outline, start writing	7 Keep writing
8 Finish first draft	9 Write bibliography, review paper, plus ask friend to read it	10 12-hour shift, no study time	11 Revise paper, proofread	12 Proofread one last time, make final copy	13 PAPER DUE	14

Ben started here and worked backward.

Ben was not a fast writer. He knew the paper would take more time than he usually spent studying. Planning ahead on the calendar helped. Ben also lined up some friends to help watch his children for a good part of the weekend. That way he could write without as much distraction.

Ben decided that fresh eyes reading the paper would be a great help. He asked a friend to read a copy of the paper. He took some of the friend's suggestions when he made his own revisions. Ben felt good about the paper when he turned it in.

Try It Yourself

Pretend you have a research paper due in two weeks. Working backward, plan the time you will have to work on your paper each day.

For more information on writing papers, see Steck-Vaughn's Start Smart Writing Strategies.

Strategy 3: Give an Oral Presentation

When you give a speech, a talk, or a lecture, you are sharing information in an oral presentation. A lot of the preparation for a speech is the same as for a test or research paper. But for a speech, it's especially important to consider your audience. What would be interesting to share with them? What would be useful?

Many people feel somewhat nervous talking in front of a group. It's important to practice a speech until you feel comfortable with it.

When getting ready for a speech, you collect the information as you would for a test or paper. You write notes on note cards. Then you have a choice. You can write out your speech with the information from your note cards. Or you can give the speech from the note cards without writing it out.

Most people find it works best to write out the speech. You don't have to read every word of it as you give it. You will have practiced it enough to have much of it memorized. Writing it out will help you if you forget or get stuck.

These steps will help you prepare for a speech:

1. **Use the introduction to get your audience's attention.** Make the topic of your speech clear at the beginning. Use the ending of your speech to remind your listeners why you are talking to them. You may want them to take action, learn more, or think about what you have said.
2. **Review and revise the speech.** Is there any way to make it more interesting to your audience? Can you find even better examples that the audience can relate to? Pretend that you are in the audience. What would you expect to learn from this speech?
3. **Practice giving the speech alone.** Say it out loud many times. If you can, say it into a tape recorder. Listening to your own voice will help you hear if you need to change your delivery. If there is a part that always gives you trouble, slow down before that part. When you have a good deal of it memorized, practice in front of a mirror. Look at your reflection as though you were the audience. Check to see that you make eye contact.
4. **Control your body language.** Use your hands only if you know exactly what they are going to do. For example, point to a chart or hold up a finger to show the number "1." Keep your feet firmly on the floor. Practice making eye contact.
5. **Control your voice.** Speak loudly. Keep your voice level. Make sure you don't rush. Speak more slowly than you think you should. Use pauses to emphasize important words and ideas.
6. **Give your speech to an audience of friends or family.** They will let you know if anything is awkward or unclear. Work on anything that needs to be improved.

Work with a Group

Plan a three-minute speech about your work or a hobby. Give your speech to your group of three to four students. Ask them to give comments about your voice and body language. Have them judge whether you spoke clearly, loudly, and slowly enough. Ask them to say whether you used body language effectively.

TIP
Be sure to write a complete beginning and ending for your speech. You will want to know exactly how you will start and finish it.

For more information on giving speeches, see Steck-Vaughn's Start Smart Communication Strategies.

Strategy 4: Take a Test

You usually present researched information in a test in one of two ways—short-answer or essay. For each, you are answering the questions asked. With short-answer, you need to boil down your answer to a complete sentence. With essay, you can write more, but you will need to cover more ground.

For more information on test taking, see Steck-Vaughn's Start Smart Test Preparation Strategies.

These tips will help you present information in a test.

- **The short-answer test**
  The questions ask for one piece of information. Answer in a complete sentence. Make your answer short. Be sure you have answered the question completely.

- **The essay test**
  These questions ask for more information than short-answer questions. First, read the question carefully. Be sure you know what it asks you to do. Next, think about what information you want to include in the answer. If you have time, jot down notes or make a quick outline. Then write your answer. Write quickly and carefully. You may not have much time to make changes.

TIP
For a short-answer, begin by restating the question as a statement. For an essay, begin by changing the question into a topic sentence.

Try It Yourself
Write the answer to this short-answer test question on the lines below.

1. What are three steps to help you prepare a speech?

....

....

....

 Think About It
What helps you overcome nervousness?

....

....

....